Black Man,
Black Woman,
Black Child

Black Man, Black Woman, Black Child

By Dara Kalima

Artwork by
Arthur A. Marsh and Dara Kalima

Illustrations by Arthur A. Marsh and Dara Kalima

First Printing, 2015

ISBN-13: 978-0692375792

For permission requests contact the publisher at: darakalima@gmail.com

Dedication

This book is dedicated to my angels Tank, Little O, Klassy K,
ESW, and MC and to my many ancestors.

This artistic expression is also dedicated to all the men, women, and children
desperately waiting for their voices to be heard.

I hope this book makes you proud!

Forward

I come to Dara's work as an Outsider. The themes, the perspectives, the experiences shared in her poems are not ones that I recognize as inherently familiar, or engrained in my own identity. Dara is a woman born in America to African ancestors; she grew up and has lived her whole life in the urban hodgepodge of color and language and culture that is New York City. I, on the other hand, am a white woman born of the descendants of farmers immigrated from rural Europe to the American Midwest. My ancestors, their histories accounted for and retold for generations, are rooted in fields and farms; and where I grew up, people's skin colors don't vary much at all. Dara's ancestors cannot be accounted for as mine can; their stories largely untold. Unlike most people of color in this country, I had the luxury of learning about racism in a classroom: I had to learn to identify and recognize deep, systemic racism and classism in America not from personal experience, but from my cushioned seat in a crowded lecture hall. As a person of color growing up in New York City, Dara's interaction with this world has differed markedly from my own.

I mention the difference in our backgrounds because Dara's poetry, although particular to her own experience, also feels both personal and universal to me--in spite of our varying histories. She writes about relationships and heartbreak; insecurity and loss; history and heritage; love and politics: resonating themes. She separates the works into five parts: Black Man, Black Woman, Black Child, Black Family and Black American. Based on one of the poems featured here, the structure of her collection is meant to bring you, through theme and subject, from the One to the Many. She begins with poems describing experiences that are largely specific to the individual in "Black Man," "Black Woman" and "Black Child," and by the time she brings us to "Black American," we are applying these themes to the larger context, from the micro to the macro. It's an important journey, and resonates profoundly at each level.

"Black Man, Black Woman, Black Child" is written by a woman whom I know and love personally, someone who truly deserves to write of her point of view and even represent, potentially, the perspectives of others. Dara has this keen sense of awareness to her surroundings; she has a fundamental gift for observation that I have never quite seen in another person. She calmly and quietly observes with a shrewd eye--a skill that is implicit throughout her poetry.

She is also, at times, frighteningly blunt. She will tell you exactly what she thinks, and allow you the freedom to take it or leave it. You'll notice this tone throughout her works, used both as a wicked sense of comedy ("Our Last Encounters aka Why I Must Be Fly") and also as biting social commentary ("a case of the ms. scotts").

She asks you to come to her book and hear her poetry as a blank canvas, setting the tone with "Let's Talk." Straight-forward and candid as only Dara can be, the poem asks us--we, the reader, and her, the author--to come together no matter our backgrounds and our perspectives and have a conversation "about our realities." It's a lot to ask. It has the tone, I'd even argue, of a challenge to us.

The publication of this collection is timely, of course, it must be noted. With the non-indictments for the senseless deaths of Michael Brown and Eric Garner, the protests in Ferguson and throughout the US, and the surrounding conversations about centuries of systemic racial injustice in America, "Black Man, Black Woman, Black Child" challenges us to question the state of things, to strip ourselves of our ingrained perspectives and backgrounds. Dara demands that we simply come to the table, lay bare, and talk.

Meg Kissel

Acknowledgements

They say it takes a village to raise a child; it has definitely taken a village to bring this labor of love to fruition. Therefore I must take the time to acknowledge the many people that supported this poet and the creation of this particular book.

Thank you to my mom, Darlene, and dear friend, Meg, for reading through the poems, providing edits, and advice. Thank you to my father Arthur for contributing to the artwork.

I must thank my brothers Cairo, David, and Ray for encouraging this artist. And I thank Sapphyra, Ena, and Kameron for giving your aunt a reason to want to make the world a bit better through words. This sense of gratitude also extends to my mentees: TR, VT, JH, SD and GC.

I thank Candace, Jen HD, Nate, and Stanley for providing guidance on the technical aspects of the book. Thank you, Charmaine, James, and Kenny for reminding me to use my resources and for keeping me on task. And I thank my former educators whether you taught me in first grade, seventh grade, high school, higher education, the arts or just in the school of life.

I have to send special thanks to all my fellow writers and poets who have penned with me, challenged me, and gave me a space on their stage to perform; this includes but is not limited to Alkamal, Mo Beasley, the College Club Crew, and The Writing Group.

Thank you cheerleaders: Amrita, Catherine, Corinne, Courtney, Cynthia, Eric, Hyacinth, Jen M, Jerry, Jim, Jose, Julius, Kesi, Marc, Paco, Rahshib, Sabrina, Symone, Tealeda, Tia, Veronica, and my Alaska, Journey, Momentum and YP families. I also thank my loving family, my dear friends, and colleagues who let me test out my work on them or have inspired me along the way; I cannot write all the names but I appreciate you dearly.

Though last on the page, above all, I give honor, praises, and gratitude to God for blessing me with the gift of word and giving me the tools to share this gift.

I hope you enjoy the book.

Contents

Black Child

Black Family

Preface

"Let's Talk"

Can we take a moment to have a deep conversation?
I want to discuss ancestries, legacies, oppression,
privilege and their repercussions. I want
to have a serious heart to heart with you because
there are emotions in every ounce of our beings
that are just begging to be shared. But
I only want to engage in this discourse if we
can both speak and listen from a point of openness.
Let's communicate with an understanding that
our individual experiences does not nullify
the other's. Can we agree that though we
may not understand each other's plight, that though
it is not our personal reality, can we agree
that our experiences can both be real?

I'd love to talk to you about how maddening it is
to only track two centuries of ancestors because
prior to that they were only property. I want
to talk about the lessons learned over breakfast.
Yes, how to cross the street and stranger danger
were part of the meal but it also nurtured
my fear of police and it came with a side of
"no matter how fair, I think the world should be,
this government was never created to empower me."

I want to share with you what it means to never be
paid equal to my fairer counterparts. I want to explain
what it is like to be silenced with terms such as angry
black woman, race baiter, race card and reverse
discrimination. These are all excuses to dismiss
my voice, they are tools of the deaf and ignorant.

I need to share what it means to experience those helpless
and hopeless nights when verdicts tell my husband, my
father, my brothers, sons, cousins and friends that their
lives are not worth much, that they are just worthless, that
their lives are worth less than everyone else. That dogs
are worth more and get justice long

1

before their brown bodies do.
I want to share with you the tears I've shed
due to all of these things, but
I need you to listen, to consider for a moment
that my life matters, that
black lives matter and that
my reality is not mere make believe or
something solely of my own doing.
And I promise to give you
the same respect, I will not turn a blind eye
to your plight but I need to know
that you too will consider mine.

So
Again
I ask
can we engage
in a discourse
from person to person, from
perspective to perspective, from
heart to heart about our realities.

Black Man

"My Unborn Son"

I shouldn't have to be afraid to have a little boy.
I shouldn't fear the day that a male child
springs forth from my body.
It should be a day full of joy, not dread or fear.
I shouldn't fear or worry about the hurt that will follow,
The hurt that is preordained simply because
he will be born with a birthmark that is target shaped.
The police will try to have his name on file before his first steps,
so that they can watch his every innocent movement,
so they can make sure he travels through
the school to prison pipeline on time.
Barely moments after having left my womb
the world will proclaim him to be at a deficit
all because he sprung out with brown skin from a brown skin mother
            whose parents were brown as well.
Every day of his life will be a fight for survival,
not just because of black on black violence
but primarily because his school will try to starve his brain,
the police will try to rob him of his sense of safety,
and media will try to destroy every bit of dignity and pride he has.
And I will have to fight every day to get him to realize
that he can be so much more,
that 21 doesn't have to mark the end of his life,
and that that hallowed hall education is far sexier than street cred even
if both are designed to leave him behind no matter how hard he tries.
I fear the day I will have to try to mend his wounds when his kin
calls him a sellout, simply because he fought for the advancement
that was promised but never given.
And I fear knowing that no matter how far he comes
a bag of skittles, new kicks, a wallet, a wrong look,
the wrong place or even winning presidency
could lead to his demise because that bullet finally found its target,
like it was his birthright.
I want a son because I believe in his potential
to be anything, to be any one
but I am terrified of the day he would arrive,
knowing all too well the challenges he will face
just because of his race.

"College Destiny?"

Doing what I did is driving me insane
Why did I behave like a silly young kid?
The guilt is infesting my heart and my brain
I cheated in a class while being tested

Why did I behave like a silly young kid?
The teacher is starting to stare at me funny
I cheated in a class while being tested
I am smart so how could I be such a dummy?

The teacher is starting to stare at me funny
If only I took the time to have studied
I am smart so how could I be such a dummy?
Why did I copy these words from my buddy?

If only I took the time to have studied
I wouldn't be questioning my college destiny
Why did I copy these words from my buddy?
Maybe they'll be nice and just give me a D.

I wouldn't be questioning my college destiny
Doing what I did is driving me insane
Maybe they'll be nice and just give me a D
But the guilt is infesting my heart and my brain.

"Destination?"

I'm running the race, running the race, running
I'm running the race, running the race, running
I'm running the race, running the race, running
Running far from where I started from

I'm running from, running from... man
don't know what I'm running from, not sure
why I'm running but I'm running the race,
I'm running the race, I am running...
I. am. running...

They say life is a race and to win you must be running,
must be running, to win the race you must be running,
must be running, but I've been running and running
been running so long, forgot why I started running all along.

I keep running, I been running, been running too
long, running too long, running so long don't
know where I'm going. I'm just running to be running.
Not seeing, not savoring, no time, got to win,
got to win the race running,
I am running the race, running the race, running

So I am running the race, running the race, running
I'm running the race, running the race, running
Running from where I started not knowing where I'm going
but I'm running the race, running the race, running.
I'm running the race, running the race, running.
I'm running the race, running the race, running
got to run to win, got to win, so I'm running.

"Peter Pan"

He was Peter Pan,
he was that boy that grew
but never quite became a man...

Upon approaching that age
that legally marks the completion
of the transition from boy to man
Peter's childish escapade began.
Though he was no longer a child
and now lived in man's land
the rebellious boy developed
his genius but misled plan...

It started simple enough,
a sip here, a taste there
an experiment from time to time
But before anyone was aware,
That boy they loved was no longer there
See, like a mischievous child in a candy store

he was soon craving much, much more
yet his desires did not exactly match his allowance
so he allowed his 5 fingers to supply the discounts

And before long the boy
that refused to be a man
was now grasped tightly
in the Blue Man's hands.

The restless soul succeeded in his goal
He was only required to do what Blue Man told.
He acquiesced to decisions about when to dress, bathe, and play.
He was free of adult burdens and could waste the days away.
He cared not about meeting ends 'cause while there was a chore or two
food and shelter were always provided no matter what he'd do.

And with this he was content.

But because being in that place
soothed the screaming child inside
in time freedom was the awarded prize...

And every time accolades were given
Peter Pan, the unwilling, struck again
proving that the boy would never die
and though in a grown body he still resided.

And after his last release
the child seemed at peace
until the temper tantrum began
and Peter formulated the master plan
at 5am he'd do the deed accidentally
forgetting to stop the squeeze.
He buried the evidence and pranced in delight
waiting for Mr. Blue to come that night.

See Peter was a fiend,
escapism his American dream.
While others hoped to one day be a man,
career, family, adulthood; they were never his plan...

"it ain't easy"

my baby bottle was filled with
murky stereotypes and stigmas
for nourishment. lullabies were
thug songs blasting from the car
downstairs and the shots outside.
so, of course my first steps
had to have the baddest swagger
worthy of demanding respect.
i really had no choice you see
being me wasn't all that easy.

classes in my formative years
included "tough & macho" levels 1-3
which were supplemented with
"how-to-avoid-crying" tutorials. i
learned how to handle hassling cops
during hands-on workshops and took
hustler (a.k.a. bread winner) seminars.
understand, i had no choice you see
growing up like me wasn't that easy.

yet, i carried on in this education
game determined to be more than
past lessons dictated, but those
hallowed halls greeted me with
contrived complex lectures explaining
how my skin shade made me less
than best. even, ladies looked down.
see, somehow by being enrolled
i managed to fail all my life lessons.
i was too proper, too nice, too clean,
and far too educated it would seem.
developing me, really wasn't that easy.

apparently, i was handicapped in utero
despite being deemed perfection in
His eyes... in their eyes, i am endowed
with so little that i wasn't just born into it but
was conceived in the struggle... 'til this day
great griots recite stories about kings that
once looked like me but currently that's
just a fantasy, so i fight twice as hard for
half as much, i, fight twice as hard, for
half as much, i fight, twice, as hard, for,
half, as much, simply trying to make it reality,
fortunately, i really have no choice you see
i am not made to quit, but man, the path to me
sure ain't easy.

"Blessings Received"

I was told enter the desert with scissors
to cut the fat from my life, name the devils,
remove the chains hindering my path to great.
I immediately obeyed, began the journey
with scissors held tightly in hand, prayer
permanently on my lips, and faith resiliently
residing in my heart. I started trimming, initially
cutting the tiniest of slithers of strife away, and
as timed passed so did the difficulty of the task,
large chunks began to fall to the side, the once
daunting burden became a wonderful game when
knowing God's greatness was to be the prize. I
was sent there, to that barren place to strip all
things blocking my path. As the piles grew my
load lightened, my prayers became stronger, my
heart started to soar and in this desert, I saw
a sight and felt a cleansing uncommon to this
dusty shore. A pillowy, soothing, healing fell
upon me, surrounding me. The harsh desert
I was sent to became a winter wonderland.
Knowing it was my reward for unwavering faith
I offered up my prayers of praise, sang joyful songs
and danced anew, reveling in blessings received.

"Steven"

He was just getting it.
After all the struggles,
Childhood abuses,
Financial problems,
Premarital children,
Rocky unions...
After all the mistakes,
The falls to the bottom,
The missteps and stumbles
He had finally found his footing.
After all the poverty,
The grief, the hurt and pain
He finally got it.
Finally picked himself up
And got things straight.
He was walking on his own.
Independent of his family
Finally learning to maintain
Sanity in this hectic hard world.
He had just found his own stride
When he walked blindly
Into the middle of the street.
He was just getting it
When he was called home.
When all his hard work
Finally seemed like
It was worth something,
That glory was here,
He was taken there...
And while I grieve for his wife,
Children, sister and the rest of his kin,
While I grieve for my lost cousin
My only comfort is in knowing
There is a plan.
Not for me to understand
But a plan all the same...
At least he finally got it.
While others still have not.
I am so proud of him
Even if he never knew,

For at the end of day
After all the battles
He kept going and got it.

"Tommy"

He wore the scent well. His body
chemistry matched the chemist's
dream so perfectly that just a waft
caused my knees to quiver and
my heart to flutter. He wore it well;
better than any that thought they could,
he was the only that should, others
stunk like skunks buried in aged trash.
He wore it well and in every instance
that I was allowed near him I became
hopelessly intoxicated. He smelled
like love, and I was deeply in love
with his scent and with him. He
epitomized "man": husky, musty, tall,
sexy, smooth, genuine and reliable and
in love with me too. Sadly, our story
was never really meant to be, time and
life tore us apart... My nostrils wept
for the loss of his scent, my heart
weeps for the loss of its equal. And
now I am doomed to walk the world
seeking the smell that won control
over all my senses, knowing I won't
succeed. I am destined to fail, after all
it was only exquisite on him, only perfectly
matched his chemistry. He wore it well.

"Kenyada"

Life is short, too short
You're alive
Then
BOOM
You're gone.
Two seconds ago
You were on the way to my door.
Three weeks ago
You got a raise at your job.
Four months ago
You graduated from school.
You were alive five seconds ago.
And in the blink of an eye
You tragically died.
Life is too short.
You proved that the other day.
Even in anticipation for it,
It comes too fast.
You were fine.
You were coming to see me
To spend time with me again
To walk with me around the lake.
Then BOOM you were gone.
My love
The love of my life
One mistake
One second
One blink you were gone
Gone too far
Gone too fast
Gone before I could say
I love you at last.

"Mr. Chivalry"

He loved women,
he loved every,
single, minute thing
about women. He
loved their hair, their
skin, their scent, their
softness, and their
moistness. He loved
women from toenail
to split ends, from
muffin tops to back
rolls. Women, were
his addiction, and boy
did he love to make
women feel like queens.
Ensuring that feet
only swept clouds, he
bathed women in meals,
salons, jewels and toys.
With him, women's only
task was getting dressed
and he even made that
easy, no matter the wear,
he clothed them in words
of beauty. He provided for
every solitary need; that is
the deed a man must do, but
this lover of women never
loved Woman, never once
surrendered completely,
was never weak, never
shared emotionally. He
simply memorized the
provider's script but failed
to appreciate the caliber
of the character. You can't
be a lover without knowing
love, can't supply love if you
know not what is required,
you can't provide if you never
understand that Woman

desires more than feigned
chivalry. Woman only wanted
him, she hungered for the real
him, longing only for that one
gift he never would give.
This master lover of women
failed at loving Woman.

"Jambar"

You are Jambar
My warrior
My king.

Taken
From
Mother
Brought
Here on a ship
Survived
This tough
Strange land.

Your legs
Are tree trunks
Rooted
In your
Ancestry.

Your arms
Are steel
Strong enough
To carry
The world.

Your head
Is a ripe apple
Fresh from
The tree
Of knowledge.

Your heart
Is a sponge
Absorbing love
From those
You hold dear.

You are
Jambar
My warrior
My one
True king.
I am blessed
To be chosen
As your queen.

"He Waited for Her"

Dear love, Hurry back to me
Were the words flowing through his head
As he thought of his love that has been delayed
She was caught in the midnight hike
Left no word to let him know she'd soon arrive
So stood this man waiting for her return
Longing to reunite with his lost love
And as the dark silhouettes turned the corner
Heading back to their shadowy homes
His heart stopped. Hoping it was her
But with the flash of a light his hope was crushed
The silhouettes were proven not to be his love
But he vowed to stand on this corner
Until his soul was reunited with its first love
He held true to his word and never wavered
Alone he stood staring at that bloodied moon
His lonely eyes filling with lost love's tears
As he waited to reunite with his fallen wife.

"A Father's Love"

During the blackout
He began to walk
Starting at 40th Street
Ending at Tremont Avenue
Over 150 blocks
He walked for me
His limbs ached
Body was in pain
Ankles screamed in agony
But he walked just for me.

"To Sir…"

How do you thank someone who has taken you from crayons to perfume?
It isn't easy… It isn't easy… It isn't easy

See Lulu sang this song to you on behalf of me, 409, and 410
Even if she, nor we, ever knew it back then

You were my sir, and though I/we were not a bunch of bad kids from
        Britain
You deposited into our educational and emotional banks so we'd never be
        poverty stricken

Your room was a home, always welcoming us with a "wuz up" spelled out
        on the board
And while I never grew to love history, in your class I was never bored.

Between the MC shuffles, backwards hats, spittle, and finger waving high
        fives
Class would always find me present and ready for some historical jive

It was you that helped to set me on the path that I am on today
By encouraging the singer/actor/dancer/poet/public speaker hanging in
        Lab's hallways

It wasn't until graduate school where I'd realize the MC/To Sir connection
While discussing how to be a pedagogue, my thoughts went in your
        direction

The mentor, role model, friend, and advocate they described was you
And the smile on your face as I told you, I wished to view

So I began to wonder...
How do you thank someone who has taken you from crayons to
     perfume?
I guess that phone call will have to do....

And while I still aim for those stars because you asked for us to reach past
     the moon
In my heart and my head I'll always hear your whimsical tune...

Ba da dadum ba da dadum ba da da da da da dadum Bat bat bada bum
     bumdum...

It saddens me greatly as I think upon this day
That I must now place your picture alongside Ebony and Kim,
My inspirations that have passed through that threshold way

But I will always sing the songs you drilled into our heads,
My feet will always rejoice and dance at the sound of the drum
My speeches and poems will always evoke global thoughts
And you, my educator and friend, will always be right there with me

So again I ask "how do you thank someone?" I did it partially with this pen
The rest will be making the best of this life I have left to spend

And while I could reminisce about
More time spent in HS and beyond
I will bring an end to this rhyme and song
And hope that you know that this was for you
To you, *To MC with love...*

"The Revolutionist"

We sat on the dusty sagging couch
and he began to tell me his story,
he spoke about immigration and
learning English. He talked about
family and community. He discussed
the racism inherent in the arts and
we spoke about the battles waged.
He raised his wrinkled left fist then
teared up as he thought of the
uncompleted dream. He spoke
of legacy and wondered if it was
all for naught, would the battle
ever be won? Who would carry on?
I saw this aged man as new and
knew my duty: carry his torch too.

"Blue and Red"

It doesn't matter if he wears
a bowtie or a baseball cap,
If he holds a PhD or a GED
If he's a minister or a hustler
Doesn't matter whether he lives
In a mansion or the projects,
Or if he drives a Bentley or a hoopty
He will always be victim to a fear
Only his brown brothers know.
He will constantly live in a
Fight or flight state of existence
No matter if it's the Queen's English
or slang he communicates with
The result can always be the same
The wrong look, the wrong words,
The slightest "threatening" gesture
Can cost him his life when
Summoned by blue and red lights.

"The Daily Battle"

There is a war waging...raging...and roaring
There is a battle brewing and he is caught in it.
He struggles between perceptions and reality.
He tussles between stereotypes and facts.
Never knowing whether or not he will be allowed
To be on the offense today or if it is his day to react.
They all wait and watch to see his move and
He watches as well, takes the temperature,
Not sure what to make of this day. The world
Is waiting for him to fail, but his family needs
Him to win, and all he desperately wants is peace.
To live like every other American, but he can't,
Black men have never been afforded that opportunity.

Black Woman

"Baby Girl"

She was their baby girl,
not just a baby but the
youngest of the tribe.
She was to be the pride
and joy, the one to be
the composite of all, the
last artifact of their
love. She was to be the
chance to make amends
and to glue the fractured
together. She was to bring
so much, she was to be
so much. So much
resided on who she'd
become, that they named
her beautiful peaceful
in hopes that she'd
inject peaceful beauty
to their kindred unit.

"The Witness"

She sat in the back seat
captive audience to the
sinister act before her.
They assumed she was
too young to notice, too
young to be but so affected,
too young to understand
their complexity. They
kept on with their game
thinking their act couldn't
possibly have an impact,
she'd never remember
the living rooms she was
left in, while they played
bride and groom, doctor
and nurse, or teacher
and student... they thought

she'd never realize that
that doll was a bribe, not
a good girl's prize. Mommy
was never to know of Dad's
tryst and he never cared
about the act's impacts,
never thought that what
daughter witnessed she'd
carry always, never
considered that she'd be
torn up about it in her
adult days... How now
will she find a healthy
love when childhood
taught only cheating?
Did they think of this
when they forced her
to witness their tryst?

"Infection"

I'm sure you thought you escaped
that by only taking a glance it was
a missed chance and nothing more...
you were wrong. I saw you peek
over your shoulder for another view.
I knew you would, see by that point
you were mine, my helpless fool, a
victim of my womanly charms, you
didn't choose for take two... I tagged
you, worked my voodoo on you from
the moment you reached my view...
there was absolutely nothing to do,
see I am infectious, with a stare your
attention is captive here... Can't you
already feel me wrapping myself
around your tongue so that you only
speak words of me? Soon your body
will be mine too, you'll be needing
my touch like it's the only thing able
to nurture your soul... The image of me
is now encompassing a sphere of

your dome and the only thought residing
is taking me home. I'd release you if
I wanted to but not yet, not now.
Just stand there paralyzed as that glance
transforms to a stare, then a fixation,
your imagination stuck on the thought of
me straddling you, and you entering there...
I know how it goes... but now is not
the time, and in moments you will find
that burning physical desire subside
as your veins rush this infection to your
beating heart... I know you can feel
the steady beat grow rapidly and all
you need is to know me, but all will come
in due time. See, I've got plans for you
ever since we crossed our views, and
my dear, there's nothing left for you to do.

"Momma's Famous Peach Cobbler"

She walked up to the door
With ingredients in hand.
She was worried
Afraid that going there
Would be a mistake.
Would they get into a fight?
They didn't always get along.
She could always buy it
In a store she thought.
No need to ask for
This woman's help.
But she knew more problems
Would arise if she cancelled.
So she rang the doorbell.
The door opened
Hey. I was wondering
If you'd make it,
The woman said.
Of course I would
I was looking forward to this.
With little more to say

They got straight to it.
They laid out the ingredients.
Decided to begin with the crust.
One sifted the flour, sugar,
Baking powder and salt into the bowl.
The other added in the
Shortening and buttermilk.
Make sure you roll the dough
Into a ball,
The wiser one said.
You know he always liked to watch me.
He just knew I was making it for him.
She said, thinking back to years ago.
Reminiscing to when
He was still her little boy
Before she lost a son
And gained a daughter-in-law.
Yes he spoke of it often
That's why I wanted your help
To make it for him for his birthday.
I wanted to give him a nice surprise.
And these few words opened up a dialogue
The two never had before.
The mom finally understood his choice.
The wife finally saw his nurturing mother.
They spoke of him, his childhood
And his many bad habits.
They discussed the stresses
Of being a new wife
As well as the pleasures of starting a new life.
They talked for what felt like hours
While baking his favorite treat
Not realizing the aroma in the air
The oven's buzzer went off
And they went to check on the treat.
When she saw the browned crust
She realized it was time to go.
The surprise would be ruined
If she arrived home late
Not wanting the moment to end,
Not wanting to leave her new mom,
She regretfully hugged her goodbye
Thanked her for all her help

And promised to stop by soon.
Packed up his mom-made peach cobbler
And headed for their home.
As she walked from the house
She was glad that she knocked on that door.
And smiled for the first time in regards to his mom
She was happy to realize that that adversary
Turned out to be a good mother-in-law.

"Realities v Perceptions"

They think she ate sour grapes,
lost her aspirations and stormed
away. That's what was perceived.
They never asked her side, never
inquired if she was okay post
the loss of her dreams, just ran
off of perceptions, made opinions on
misconceptions. They held bitterness
against her not knowing how bitter
life had been to her, just assumed
they knew the story of her departure,
thought her vows of love and loyalties
were just lies, didn't know about the
disloyalty and lacking love shown to her.
They just simply assumed that she
was not who she claimed to be, just
one who spun opportunistic stories.
But they never inquired as to why
she fell back, never considered that she
might have been given no choice but
to fall. Never asked why she faded
to black, never asked if she was ok. They
never cared about her side, only the parts
they could see with their eyes. If only
they'd have asked why, would they then
apologize for how they persecuted her,
isolated her, added hurt upon her hurt?

Who now might be brave enough
to look past their misguided perceptions
and ask her even one of the questions?

"Can't Care"

I hope that you forgive me
but I need to say this, I need to
get this out of me and into
the open air while you are here.

I know I'm your friendly therapist,
that confidant you share your endless
thoughts and feelings with. And I
always seem to happily oblige,
to grab a chair, listen. I'll advise and
pose challenges but now I have to
tell you this and I ask that you

understand this...
I don't care.

I don't. I never really have. I mean
I care to the extent in which you
clearly care but I'm tired of pretending
like any of this shit matters to me.
It doesn't. None of it does.

I don't care about what tiles
you choose for your kitchen.
I don't care about your employee
perks or your weekend excursions.
And I'd like to tell you that I sorta
feel bad telling you this, but truthfully
I don't. I just don't care. I can't.

I can't care anymore because there
are other things to be concerned about.
Yes, times are hard and you want to cry
because you didn't get a raise but
I can't make ends meet on my check,

I have friends who are barely
making minimum wage and others
are rubbing unemployment checks together
trying to get a glimmer of that American dream.

I know you are yearning for the comfort
of your old neighborhood but I have a friend
living in a friend of a friend's barbershop
and I have another over there threatening
to commit suicide. And while I don't care
to listen to him tell me about yet another
attempt he plans on taking I care about
the fact that he's so lost that he sees eternal
darkness as the only way out. I spend
half of my time praying that he doesn't
follow through on his threat again and
so sorry but I have no more "you" time to spend.

And while to some the acquisition
of new wheels matters, it doesn't to me.
My mind is preoccupied with the woman
I once worked with at a prison alternative.
Has she finally gotten it together? Gotten a job?
A place of her own? Found productive ways
to address her painful story, full of
a lifetime of abuse? Or has she
headed back into the system on account of
missteps she was destined to repeat?

And so while you rambled on about
your social status again, I just can't care.
Mostly because every day I'm haunted
by the ghosts of my ancestors that are
saddened by the images of modern day
niggers, those stereotypes my brothers
and sisters continuously perpetuate,
when my kin was killed to prevent
such a fate. Yes, we are owed, payment
is past due and if tomorrow I could,
I'd go to those steps and demand
retribution for this generations long debt
owed to my family for all the crimes

against humanity committed in the name
of purity... but I can't and despite how much
I try to lead by example and show them that
we can be more, to prove to them that we
need to stop embracing a label designed
to imprison our souls and limit our destinies,
that we need to stop naively embracing
an identity that was never ours, I haven't. It saddens,
it frustrates, it angers me to know in that task somehow
I still fail, that we are still failing, even with
one of us running the house, no longer as
cleaning crew or wait staff but as
chief resident... this eats at me.

And as you go on and on about your
latest romantic interest and ask for counsel
during your wooing process, my focus shifts,
my mind wanders and then wonders if
I can ever be whole again, whole enough to
welcome Love's love again... I'm never certain
that the aches I've suffered shall heal,
that I will ever again enjoy the pleasures of
companionship, yet I still come back
to the topic at hand, you, and I focus
just long enough to advise again...

I'm sure all of this is new, but
have you ever asked, ever cared
about my load? No...
yet I still was there...

But right now I need you to know this,
and except it as truth, my truth,
I must address my own burdens,
focus in on my own tribulations and deal
with the things that truly matter to me.
And if I am to heal and to really help others,
I can no longer afford to care for you.

"A Heavy Weight"

After she methodically removed the uniform,
and after she carefully undid the harnesses
that bound her, but before her comforting
attire embraced her, she crumbled to her knees.
She, in her brownness, begged for mercy as
the weight of it all began to asphyxiate her. Her
feeble frame reverted to fetus as the levies faltered
and the malignant river coursed down her face.

"The Longest Shower"

I cover myself in soap,
And I scrub,
And scrub,
And scrub.
I scrub until my skin is red.
Then I turn the water off.
And step out of the shower.
And it all rushes back.
All the pain.
The hurt.
The misery.
The tears.
The images.
The pictures of two bodies.
Neither of them mine.
But one of them yours.
Then begins the questions:
Was she good?
Did she please you like me?
Better than me?
Did you make her moan?
Make her groan?

Did she scream your name?
Did you scream hers?
Was it good?
Was it your best yet?
Did you ever think of me?

Or was it so good,
That you no longer crave me?
Do you love me?
Do I love me?
Then all the dirt.
The grit.
The nastiness.
The filth.
It all rushes back.
And before I can even dry off,
I step back in.
I start the ritual again.
Soap covering me.
Cleaning me.
And I continue.
I scrub.
I scrub.
And scrub.
And scrub.
Maybe one day
I'll finally be clean.

"Despite"

Despite
my best
effort I
can not
not be
her.

"Apologies"

No one asks anyone
who was mugged
to apologize for
being attacked. But
everyone demands
apologies from her
for being raped. She
will not apologize.

"a case of the ms. scotts"

i have a case of the ms. scotts... no, i will not belt out a powerhouse tune. this is not a beautiful love song though it is about love or more so the lack thereof. and i am not here to compete over some man and there is no need for me to recite to you how much deeper and flyer my love is because i already know that you didn't care to know this, because you didn't take the time to notice. and that is why i have the case of the ms. scotts.

like jill, i am that woman that maya described; not a model's fashion size but a phenom all the same, operating only with the utmost class and charm but you divert your view like looking at me will do you harm. you hoped i wouldn't notice but how could i not know this and this is why i have the case of the ms. scotts...

by now you are wondering what that entails, maybe your memory only recalls the confident (and slimmer) actor, poet, and singer. maybe you forgot that before the spotlights she was just a voluptuous natural woman. before you gave a damn about who she was, before the world labeled her a beauty, she felt compelled to hide... not because she was ashamed, she owned her talents and already claimed her space in this world but she was also acutely aware of what it is you'd typically like to view, so rather than kill a budding career she didn't dare show her face there. she had to cater to your superficialities, massage your brain, whet your senses, and beat on your eardrums all in the name of getting you caught up in her before you got caught up in her lack of the typical. she knew this. i know this... and hence why i have a mean case of the ms. scotts.

see, i don't care what you look like. whether you are short and fat or tall and lanky it really doesn't matter as long as you can make love to the folds of my brain, then you will certainly drive me insane and be the one to blame for the sugary sweet trail i'd leave behind at every venue i visited. and by then you'd have long noticed how deep this love is. and honestly the entire the world would know this, but you couldn't get past what society has deemed beautiful to see the true beauty that is me and this is where the ms. scotts set in.

it entered the scene just in time for that dramatic pause, and that familiar yet sudden silence reverberated in my inbox and deflated my heart. you know that silence, that silence that came right after i sent you a sexy yet classy pic just to give you a quick peek at the physical beauty that is me.... that silence that almost makes me want to lie and say "na i don't have a picture, my computer died as did all images of me so sorry dear you can't see" but why would i? i like ms. am not ashamed, i'm just tired of your prepubescent ideologies on what a woman like me is "supposed" to be. that is not me, and actually, i surpass that conceptuality. i am just simply fatigued from having to subject myself to your ignorance but at least now i know that you are not mr. right, mr. right-now, or mr. right-now-is-fine-because-i've-got-nothing-better-to-do. i'm grateful in the long run that our story is through but i admit to being spent, depleted from this game, and though the day after tomorrow i'll again be noticed, i must admit to knowing this, i have currently but temporarily come down with a case of the ms. scotts.

"Un-Claiming Cute"

"C", ca, ca, candy, cover, crazy
And then "U", oooo, uhhhh,
Ca, ca uooo cooo cool, cougar, cue
Then "T", ta, ta, tasty, texture, tease,
Then back to "C", caaa uuu ta ta
Ca uu tt... Cut, Cute?

See I can't embrace the word "cute"
Like Eve Ensler embraced cunt,
She took the word claimed it,
And renamed it, from the insult
It was, but "cute?"...

How does one take what seems harmless
And transform it to a positive?...

Cute?
Cute is... babies, adorable,
Innocence, soft, fluffy, sweet, puppies,
It's teddy bears, and cabbage patch kids,
Cute is something you want to grab and snuggle with.
Cute is that guy you sorta dig, it's that
Joke that was almost funny, that thing that
Only slightly grabbed your attention.
But cute for many years has been my definition
And trust me; it has not been by choice
But by those that are too deaf to hear my voice.

I am that girl that's typecast as friend.
The "cute" label always marking my end.
See, she's just not my cup of tea. She just doesn't have the sexy womanly edge.
No spark or zest, just adorable... She's cute. Yep that's it. That's what she is...
And though admittedly sometimes
I play the child card just to lay it on thick,
So that I could get my way but
That's not who I am every single day.

There are times when my man
Gives me that look signaling wassup
Then from his tasty lips slips
"You are so cute I just want to eat you up"
I become violently nauseous
Wanting to run to the can and puke.
And after giving back my food I ask:
How do you like me now? Am I still cute?

I am not a fuzzy little thing that
Momentarily peaks your interest
When I sashay into a room
All know I've made an entrance
I am a lady that does everything with style
My unique touch makes everyone smile
I am mature, ambitious, and well-mannered,
I'm so good I exceed every standard
I nurture and support all of those around me

I hide the stress so well that no-one can see.
I am too good to be found just on anyone's arm
I even greet enemies with a special kind of charm
I do not neglect my roles or any duty
Though you only see cute rather than beauty.

See cute equals young, inexperienced and naïve
But in that definition you won't find the real me.
I am a woman with a body to bring life to the world,
You'd get lost in the net that I could have twirled.
I give birth to inspiration, hope, love, boys and girls,
And baby, I have all the womanly curls,
My face may be round my body a little plump
But I will school you while doing the bump.
I could drive the sanest wild, make the untamable mild
If only they'd take the time to see me as more than a child.
But they must first get past their prepubescent views
On what a woman is and what she should do.
I bring knowledge and wisdom well surpassing my stage
But with that one word you act as if I'm half your age.
I can provide you with all that you may possibly wish
And I even may surprise you with some special tricks
But if I am referred to that way once again
My sweet dear, you will never get a spin.

See a woman is more than just an idealized doll,
And beauty is defined as more than svelte and tall.
I am devoted, giving, loving and wise,
And my baggage is only purse size
And though innocent I may look
A step you just mistook.
'Cause "cute" and I just can't be,
It's not my label, so don't stick it to me.
While Eve can do pieces on reclaiming cunt
With a caa and an uhhh and nnnasty tttouch
Here and now I've decided to abolish that word
'Cause this beautiful, black woman has just had too much.

"Her Black History"

She held the dusty programs intensely reading
Learning about those ancestors that passed
Newly inspired by their legacy of succeeding
Setting goals in hopes they'll be surpassed

She understood her future by looking into the past
Stories of men and women, she was needing
Their strength, their lives, are hers to carry at last
She held the dusty programs intensely reading

He was a minister, she a supervisor, both leading
She lawyer, he entrepreneur, breaking the cast
Others protesting for rights they were pleading
Finally, learning about her ancestors that passed

Individual lives, various tales, in her time amassed
The lost history, from identity was always impeding
But these documents finally connecting the vast
Newly inspired by their legacy of succeeding

But all families have skeletons worthy of heeding
Some buried tales of ancestors made her aghast
Brothers killing brothers over loves toxic feeding
Yet they still set goals hoping they'd be surpassed

She found the link to which she could hold fast
Having learned of a legacy worthy of repeating
Future no longer limited, free to release her mast
With them as her wind, it's time for her proceeding
She anew, thanks to the dusty programs...

"At 30"

I found my voice,
and used it, I
no longer laid
on my back taking
whatever caustic
lovers delved out.
Their acidic sweat
burning away my
self-esteem as they
worked hard to
build up theirs.

I was no longer
going to be their
inflatable toy, filled
with hot air and used
only for their release
then tucked away,
hidden and neglected.

I realized I was
so much more, so I
finally stood up,
nursed my burns, filled
myself with attention,
love and appreciation,
fortified the parts
they tried so
desperately
to destroy.

Then I confronted
my maker, addressed
their faults that they
subsequently ingrained
during my manufacturing.
This faulty apprentice
created me with a flaw
which led to my heart
being compromised and

hungry before I ever
developed awareness.
And this created
the emptiness lovers
used to exploit

but no more.

I was no longer this
plastic toy. At 30
I became master
of my fate, allowing
no one to deflate me
or needing no one
to help me inflate
myself for that matter.

I found my voice,
used it, and would
not let another ever
abuse it or refuse
it again. At 30, I
finally started seeing
the me they tried
to destroy and I finally
started loving myself.

"Our Last Encounters aka Why I Must Be Fly"

At our last encounter
before hello could exit your lips,
"it smells like piss"
were the words you greeted me with.
It seems that my choice in outdoor seating
while waiting for your tardy self was poorly chosen
and you felt compelled to tell me as much.

As I put the scarf that I was making away,
so that you could have my full attention
you replied "couldn't you just buy one?"
You were never impressed with my craft.

But I let your negativity pass
opting to have a good time.
During dinner I inquired about your new phone.
Without thinking or even listening
you adamantly proclaimed
that I saw it during the last date,
but what you meant was
the other chick that you called me complaining about
and now confused me with, saw it that day.

And I only slightly hinted
at the inappropriateness
of the image of some unrelated lady
that you placed as the backdrop on your new toy.
But hey it's your phone, and I wasn't your girl,
you weren't my guy,
so what say had I?

But boy was I relieved when
you pointed out that we were just
"really
good
friends,"
that the romantic story of us was now at an end.
So I treated you like a friend,
I stopped contacting you daily,
I ceased making plans because
I stopped treating you like my prospective man.

But even though that is what you stated
my disinterest wasn't appreciated.

And in retaliation you
threw my rape
in my face
like it was something I
had to apologize to you for.
I'm finally over apologizing to myself,
I apologize no more.
So why do I owe you one?
You were no one,
nothing more than a bystander

caught in the emotional line of fire years ago.
And I apologized back then, but you just can't let it go.
If anyone doles out an apology,
if any is going to say the words, "I'm sorry"
it is you who owes me
for never getting past yourself
to care to ask how I ever felt.

But you've always been one classy dude.
And I'm glad your class is gone.
But this piece, this poem really isn't
about bashing you, it's how
I came to realize just how fly I am.
And my oh my,
how fly am I!

How do I know I'm fly?
Well
I just am but
you prove it every time you come back.
Every time you text, you IM,
you try to connect and then you follow me
you prove it to yourself and to me.
The constant question asked is
what do you do with your life now that I'm gone,
but asking me that question is where you've gone wrong.
I thought my silence was a loud enough reply,
Sweetie,
I stopped caring about what you do when you said goodbye,
yet, you, return still
trying to fill a void you instilled.

Considering how
unappealing
you once said I was,
I wish my fly could be more repelling
so that you'd finally go away but you won't,
it's really that you can't.
and even though I clearly don't want you,
you can't help but to try,
after all you yourself have proven it;
I'm just that fly!

Black Child

"A Child's Question?"

Why are there candles?
Birthday cakes must make a wish
With no fire where would wish go?

"Friends"

Friends are caring.
They don't mind sharing.
They treat you nice.
They don't treat you with a heart of ice.
They are very fair.
They are always there.
With you they talk.
And sometimes go for long walks.
The time together is fun.
They even stick together in the warm hot sun.
Friends brighten the day,
In every way.

"You Are My Best Friend"

You are the best friend a friend should be
You are nicer than anyone could be

When I am sad you bring me joy
When I'm lonely you bring me a toy

You are my sunshine when my day is cloudy
You are my smile when I don't feel too smiley

You were there for me when I was sad
You were my happiness when I was mad

What I am trying to say
Is without you, I couldn't make it through the day

I want you to know you're my best friend
And that I hope you are, until the end

"Moments Lost"

I nostalgically look at a picture
I took at the age of eight
It's completely out of focus
It's a picture of the slanted
View outside my window but it included
The dirty cream flowered curtains, the
Large Venetian blinds that were clumsily
Pushed to the side. My life size
Hairstyle Barbie head sits
On the windowsill with dusty books
And with one of my sisters odd art projects.
The window needed to be washed
And the child safety bars obstructed
What little view of outside there was.
There was no composition, I just wanted
To capture the view from my window
On my 110mm yellow Cabbage Patch camera.
And though today the picture made no sense
Back then I was ecstatic when I had enough money
To pay for the film's developing. Pride filled me
From all those masterful pictures I had taken.
I look back at them now and laugh
But am glad that those were taken before
For if those were done in this digital age
Those memories would have simply been erased.

"At 10"

I cornered my guy under the stairs
and stole my first kiss but rumors
spread that I was a lesbian, which
was a word I only learned then. I
was voted out of a club I proudly
created and it was around then
that sadness crept in. I didn't have
words or understanding but knew
joy wasn't to be mine, at least not
in my abode. But it was also then

that my passion for sign language
kicked in. And I had already penned
a few poetic pieces by then but
never knew this year was when
who I would be today once began.

"Ex-Friend"

We used to be friends,
But now it ends.
You're very cold and I don't need it anymore.

What ever happened to the way it was?

We used to be close
But now I'm closing that door.

For nine years we've known each other so long
We used to hang on the phone

All my troubles they come from you
Now it's over
Our friendship is through.

"The Awkward Child"

No-one plays with the awkward child
They pick and prod at the single soul
The rain from one can flood the world
Alone in the world they start to roam

They pick and prod at the single soul
In a crowded room no-one is there
Alone in the world they start to roam
Standing on a cliff. Looking outside in.

In a crowded room no-one is there
In the desert land grows a pretty rose
Standing on a cliff. Looking outside in.
Blossoming to a woman from young girl

In the desert land grows a pretty rose
The end of rain means the end of the storm
Blossoming to a woman from young girl
Realizing assurance was needed in vain

The end of rain means the end of the storm
The unique child proudly stands alone
Realizing assurance was needed in vain
Acceptance of self, brought a brighter day

The unique child proudly stands alone
No-one plays with the awkward child
Acceptance of self, brought a brighter day
Rain has stopped. No more flooding world.

"At 13"

My world revolved around Red.
Red was his favorite color and
he was my favorite guy. I wrote
middle school sized love letters
to him placing my heart on page,
And at the coaxing of others and with
a three-wayed audience, I read
it to him one night and his reply
was to dedicate a tune to me.
"I'd Die Without You" was our song.
It was the song that confirmed
that he held a torch for me even
if it was dimmer than the light
my heart exuded. I spent evenings
glued to the phone talking him off
the newest ledge hoping he'd
instead leap for little ole me. I
loved me some Red like those
with oral fixations love them some
Wrigley's Big Red chewing gum.

I'd chew over thoughts of him day
and night. He was skinny, scrawny
skinny but that bothered me none.
He had perfect caramel skin, a
smile that melted my heart and
a bullet between his lovely lips.
Never fully sure why he walked
around with it but he always held
it by his lips in class, and I'd stare
at it and at him as time passed. I
suppose it was his sense of security
and his tie to the street. It was
part of the stories he'd mention
in passing during his tales about last
night's activities. But thug or not, I
fully embraced Red and hoped he'd
embrace me too...October came
I scrounged up the nerve to ask
him to be my Halloween Party date.
He replied that as long as his girl
didn't go he'd be all mine. And
with this I was totally fine, until life
sideswiped me and my plans. Party
night was designated as the time that
mom and I packed, making a quick
exit from our hell...that was the night
Red was finally going to be under my spell...

...As I placed my life in boxes, I
wondered about the might have,
could have and should have been's...

Red is grown and finally married and
that crush I had has long been buried.
We catch glimpses once in a blue.
Friends share updates on what is new
but at 13, Red was my complete world
and I was oh so close to being his girl.

"At 16"

He was already 6'1
with a two year old
and was living the life
of a Latin King. This
bothered me none.

He was half black
but mostly Dominican.
His blond hair led
to constant asks if
he was Rodman and
we'd laugh it off.

He was my favorite
secret. Boyfriends
weren't allowed so
we'd meet after class
and he'd be my escort.
This gorgeous man
escorted me home.

I was in a daze the first
time his lips touched mine.
He leaned in, I met him, then
boarded my bus. Later
I'd asked did that happen
and he chuckled at my
amazement. But I was
truly amazed and dazed
by the fact he kissed me.

He chose me. He invested
in me when it could have
been any other chick. When
he could have had any other,
I was the chosen prize.
But what melted my heart
was his love of her. His
passion for fatherhood was
like none I'd seen, none I'd felt.

It was admirable. And I'd
eat up every story shared
about them. His life began
and ended with his baby girl
and yet he still made a place
in his world for me. This
couldn't be my reality,

Could it be?
It would not be.

Circumstances pulled us
in separate ways yet I still
reminisce about the days...
I think on the lessons taught.
But all that remains is one
picture, a few letters, a nose
for Hilfiger's Tommy and
treasured memories. He
was my entire world
at 16.

"Just An Average High School Day"

Morning.
Wake up.
Pack bags.
All ready,
But too early to go.
I guess I'll watch "The Grind"
I can't believe my brother likes this!
"Bye Mom!"
Okay
Enough of this,
Time for cartoons.

First class.
Study hall.
Which book should I read
I suppose my Greek book
My professor will probably discuss it today

That's done.
Mr. I wants me to join his group.
While they're reading this short story.
Oh this is deep
But I overheard the end
In my other study hall

Lunch.
Finally.
I'm starved.
Dag I'm too late
There's a long line
Just to get French fries.
It's about time
I've been waiting ten minutes
To get some food.
Back in the cafeteria
My friends are talking
About this party I could not go to
Because of family responsibilities
That's cool though
I'm glad they had fun.

Back to class.
Math.
Oh my goodness
We have a test
I completely forgot
I am utterly bored now
Nothing to do but stare at the wall
Waiting for the bell to ring
I'm watching them take their test
I'm done
The first one actually
I hope I did well.
I did rush through it.
I'm just watching
Some people work hard and struggle
While others cheat.
What a shame
To each his own, though.

I know what I did
And will pass because of it.
I wonder what class I have next.
I don't care.
As long as we don't have another test.
Yes!!
The teacher said I did well.
See how honesty pays off.
Watch, they will get older
And not be able to comprehend
Simple arithmetic.
What a shame.
I will be somewhere
While they will be nowhere.
Yes!!
Class is finally over!

Next class.
Chemistry.
I hope we will learn today.
But in all
I guess you can say
It's just another
Average high school day.

"A Letter to the Pres"

Dear Mr. President,
What are you trying to do to me?
You publicly say that the *youth* needs a better education,
Yet you allow
Our good teachers to be taken away,
Our classes enlarged,
Our transportation money disappear,
And, to top it off
You put more police officers on the street to help straighten out
And lock up us, *troubled* juveniles

Well, maybe we wouldn't be so troubled,
If, some REAL politicians, *unlike you* thought:
    Hey, one day they will govern us.
    I hope they don't show the same disrespect to us,
    That we did our elders...
    Maybe we should create smaller classes
    With GREAT teachers,
    And the BEST materials.
    That way it makes them want to stay in school
    Rather than on the street,
    And the best part is,
    We won't waste ALL the money
    On the police!

"Look at Me"

Look at me!
Helllllooooooo!!!
Look, at me!!!
I'm right in front of you,
Why can't you see me?

Don't just walk around me,
Notice me!
Hey, wait a minute,
You just walked around me?!
That means...
You do see me!
You're just ignoring me.
That's a step up.
I guess
Now all I have to do
Is convince you
To converse
With me.

"Smothered Anger"

I want to scream
I want to scream so loud
My anger shatters your eardrums
Leaving you bleeding and in pain
Wondering why?
Why did I do that?
What could you have possibly done
To drive me so insane?

I want to yell
To yell at the top of my lungs
I need to yell to release the tension you've caused.
The tension you've caused
By simply being you.

I want to bash, crash, break, destroy,
Everything you hold dear.
Maybe then you'll realize
You shouldn't have done what you did.

I want you to suffer
To be put through long, hard, pain filled torture.
Torture that has you on your knees
Begging my forgiveness
Even though you still may not know
What it is that you did.

I want you to feel the frustration
The desperation,
The pain,
The agony
I feel.

Then
And only then
May you possibly understand
How strong the urge is to kill
To hurt, to destroy
When denied the power
To utter a sound.

"Lost Hula Hoop"

The clouds streamed the tears
my heart refused
to realize on that day,
that day my hula hoop was
torn from the delicate grasp
of my tiny hands and
dusty adult artifacts
were exchanged in its place.

Coarse gray hairs infested,
slowed, and grayed
my fruitful flowering mind;
all part of the sinister
cyclical game where
innocence and freedom
are stealthy stolen, and
the ticking only remains.

The clock takes
with every tock,
playtime was destined
to melt away.

That unnatural transition
began when the clouds
streamed and screamed
on that dreary soggy day, on
that day that my hula hoop
was painfully stripped away.

Black Family

"Black Man, Black Woman, Black Child"

Black Man

Overworked, underpaid
Working hard to make minimum wage
He struggles to put food on table and clothes on child's back
And no one seems to give the man any slack
Carries the world on his shoulders and doesn't know how to share his pain
And soon all the pressure will drive him insane

Black Woman

Works hard to fulfill the strong black woman image
But more often than not her spirit gets damaged
While taking care of child, man and self
She forgets to nurture her mental health
No one but Woman can understand the pain she feels
It's not possible for anyone else to walk in her heels

Black Child

Miseducated in so many ways
And they can't understand the price their parents pay
They see all and know all but are not heard
So they go and obey someone else's word
Only they can see how badly they are frustrated
But in their parents' head their story they never registrated

Black Man, Black Woman, Black Child

Why are they the way they are?
Why does the future for them seem so far?
Why must they all wear lonely scars?

They all have goals which they wish to achieve
But they need each other to succeed
And without the support they need
Their dreams, they will never achieve.

"Smitten"

I am smitten
Not only once
But twice bitten
By cupid's arrowhead
Before this bite
My heart was dead
The shriveled
Hardened rock
Was rejuvenated
By a romantic spark
And now like my cheeks
It is red and fully flushed
Just the thought of you
Makes me blush
I once walked around
In a sadly singular spell
When it came to prospects of love
I seemed destined to fail
But then, I felt that tender prick
And cupid's magic worked
Quite quick, my eyes
Landed on you, a sweetly
Enticing yummy view
My eyes feasted
the moment we greeted
Even my heartbeat
rapidly speeded
I feel like a kid with a crush
not knowing what to do
Do I write a love note or
Do hit you with my shoe
All that I want is a few
moments of your attention
The feelings I have,
I promise not to mention
I just want to sit, talk,
chew the fat for a few
Learning all about
what you've been through
See, right now I want things

to progress slowly
Taking the time
to explore this totally
I admit that I am smitten,
and by cupid's arrow bitten
And apparently on this thing
called love I'm not quittin'
But my life has been full
of damaging days
So I just want to do this
the correct way
Please let me know
if this at all entices you
So that we can stroll
this road anew
And maybe in time
we will both be bitten
And a new chapter for us
can be written, 'cause
it'd be nice if you,
like I, was smitten.

"The Story of This Poet and That Poet"

I met this man because he was poet,
because I am a poet and this poet
wanted to chew on his brain, nibble
on his talent, ingest just a little crumb
of inspiration that would possibly
bring me to a newer level.

This poet wanted to meet that poet
so that he too could learn from me,
that he could read my words, see how
I play and then apply this game to his.

This poet needed to meet that poet
but upon contact I found walls. Walls
and more walls. Rules and barricades
making it impossible to meet and feast.
So jaded and protected in his twenty

few years that the poet eluded me. He
ran from contact... He engaged in contact
but always from afar, always distant
from the possible people interaction.
Always silent and analytical, always
methodic in his approach. He moved
like a poet spoke like a poet dressed
like the deepest individual on the planet.

At twenty-few he lived 5 lives, 5 phases
of the man that he has come to be, at
twenty-few he'd seen so much and found
his purpose far earlier than most but
robbed himself at the same moment.

Life is too serious to not be serious he said
life is too serious to not be serious, life is
too serious to not be serious was his
only response to me. This was his motto
in life, was what he lived by, but he robbed
himself, sealed his fate forever on his poetry.

See life is too serious to be too serious
you cannot live it from the distance, cannot
watch the show from the balcony, cannot
truly engage with people from inside
a plastic bubble. How can you love if you
do not let love enter in? You cannot mask
your lack of love in love poems about your
first kiss with a spliff. You can't write
about love from the perception of what
you've seen it do to others if you've never
felt that tingle run through your insides, felt
the butterflies hatch in your belly, felt your heart
beat just a bit deeper... How can you write about it?

How can you write about the long warm
embrace you had with someone that you
never had? How can you describe experiences
and emotions that you vulcanize? A Vulcan
cannot write a love poem. They can
only write whispers of pon far, they can

only write from afar they can only
write as observers. This poet challenged
that poet to be more engaged.

But that poet taught this poet something too.

This poet realized that in her analysis of that poet
that she is too detailed and fails to see the situation
in its entirety. That this poet was so focused
on the finest detail, on capturing whatever
true love felt like that she failed to explore how
vast love was, failed to see that the love of ganja
is no less important that the love of kin.

That poet taught this poet that she should
embrace the larger picture, should explore
the multitude of layers of what love and life could
include. This poet started to see that her finiteness
left her boxed in while his exploration locked him out...

And it became clear what I felt upon first contact,
what I knew I needed when we greeted. This poet
needed that poet and that poet needed this. This
poet knew that that poet was the key
to her poetry, and the she was the lock to his.

He yin. I yang. He observer. I engager.
And that is the story of he and me and our love of poetry.

"The Music Has Stopped"

The band has packed up.
The decorations were ripped down.
The party has ended.
The festivities are over.
But they are still dancing,
Dancing to the music in their heads.
The beautiful music they still remember.
They dance.
Clinging to each other,
Hanging on for dear life.

They think that maybe if they keep dancing
The band will start playing again.
There will be music once again
But the band is gone.
The party has been over for a long while
But the two keep dancing,
Hoping and praying,
That there will, be music again.

"Round 3"

The bell rings
Thus begins round 3
The stakes are higher
Our words are now quicker and hit harder than our fist
In this round the blows come with ease
And are fueled with more hate
Our fists may do the swinging
But the words do the cutting
Leaving scars that won't disappear
Making wounds that may never heal
How did we get into this match
We started as lovers on a swing
Now we are boxers in a ring
If one wins, we lose
We know this yet
We keep lashing out
Like we're pawns in someone else's games
But we are not
It's our game
Our war
And with every punch we throw
The further apart we grow
I don't like this ring
I again want my heart to sing
Can we go back to being lovers on the swing?

"His Greatest Regret"

He was his pride and joy
And all he ever wanted
Was to teach him
The definition of man
But mom and dad couldn't
Agree on anything post conception
Yet they were bonded and
He was determined to remain,
To be a presence, to be more
Than a donor or a check.
He tried to be present but she
Was determined otherwise,
And rather than expose Baby Boy
To their incessant fighting,
He walked away, becoming
What he refused to be,
Because she refused him
Stubbornly denying him.

"Choices to Make"

He made choices, his addiction
made choices, and she pays.
Yearning for nothing more than
Daddy's embrace she instead
embraces the picture, and dreams
of him. Dreams of his hug but
the dream always results in her
pressed against a glass with dad
trapped on the other side. He's never
fully within her grasp, just an image
just outside of her reach. He's just a raspy
voice on the phone from time to time.
He hears her pain hidden under
the joy during their brief call and
he aches for her, he aches for
himself. A child was all he ever wanted
but he made choices, his addiction
made choices, and they are both

paying the price. Instead of being
a constant presence in her life, he
gets to see how she grows
only when the next picture arrives,
when the next call is arranged. But
the term isn't for life, and he will
be free again and will have more
choices to make, the first being
will his addiction get the voice of choice
again or will his love for Baby Girl win?

"Her Great Cross"

She sat in bed hugging her bear
Dreaming of love she wished was there
Longing love from dad
Thinking she was bad
Always sad, lacking cheer.

He was busy, off in the bar
From family, always too far
Living for next drink
Of child, did not think
In eye blink, he left scar.

As she aged, hole in her heart grew
Searching for love, but none was true
Lacking healthy spark
Seeking dad in dark
Cold and stark, all she knew.

With his wife's love, he plays charades
Other women still he parades
Unaware of trails
Caught in telling tales
Daughter's hell, belief fades.

As an adult, in love she's lost
His choices became her great cost.
She learns how to see
Past what he showed she
Soon will be, free of cross.

"My Mommy"

My mommy is a strong beautiful woman
She's taken real good care of me
(Without the help of a man)
She works all day and comes home
And cooks dinner for me
Helps me with my homework
And when that's done we go to bed
So that she can wake up to go back to work
Her only recess is behind her eyelids
My mommy is a strong black woman
She's provides it all for me
With a smile and no frown
She's mommy and daddy,
Friend and teacher.
She is everything to me.
She is black beauty.
She is what I hope to be.

"Grandmothers"

What are grandmothers for?
Are they for knitting your clothes?
           No, of course not.
Then what are they for?
           They're for giving you help with stuff,
           Standing by you always when you need them,
           For taking you on trips,
           They take care of you when you are sick,
           And my favorite thing is when they give you money.
Oh, so that's what grandmothers are for.
No wonder I love my grandmother.

"Joseph L. Huger"

Grandpa,
What will we do without you
Who will tell those wonderful stories when dinner is through
Now that you're gone who will be the family glue

For many years we knew that the clock was winding down
But you came home and showed the doctors, that you couldn't be kept down

Then one day you told us that you needed to sleep
And left the family here, alone, to weep

I love you Grandpa, and I'm glad that you're not in pain
But wish this pain in my heart wasn't driving me insane

Please know that without you, life will never be the same
And know I'm proud of having your blood to claim

My only wish was that we had more time
Only now do I understand the truth inside your rhyme

I wish I had talked to you when glass was full of sand
But in my childish youth, I couldn't see past my hand

I can't explain the joy, to the world, your presence brought
Only recently did I realize how much, to me, you could have taught

But the lessons you did teach
I will keep close to me and within reach

Grandpa, I love you and even though you, I can no longer see
Please know no matter what, you will never die inside of me

"From Auntie to Niece"

Every time I see you I notice how you've grown
Soon you'll be a teen then a woman on her own
Before time moves too fast I had to tell you this
Being your auntie has filled my life with bliss
You make your family happy and extremely proud
We climb tops of mountains and shout out loud
Of the pretty girl we have watched grow a bit older
And now how she's her baby sister's shoulder
You've learned to protect us all with karate
And you swim so fast that we can hardly see
Though you love to play and have tons of fun
You know it isn't time until homework's done
Though we now live several states apart
I think of you often and you are in my heart
Never stop being the sweet Sapphena I know
Great things will come if seeds you now sow
Never forget to let God be your guiding light
Always do what your conscience says is right
Soon you'll be a teen, then a woman on her own
But know Auntie's proud of how you have grown

"A Tribute to My Big Sis"

She was always a trailblazer, a pioneer,
Though I longed for sister, not leader
But the difference in our ages
Set up this complex dynamic.
She lovingly mothering me,
I using her as an alliance.
As I matured it was certain
That we'd grow to see eye to eye
But time was not on our side.
So now I am left missing her,
Never getting to know her as equal
Only remembering her as Mommy 2.
And the feeling of robbery grew into rage
But in church a realization was made.
She was a trailblazer, forging the way
Taking siblings and friends under her wings,

66

Defending us from life's many bends.
But leadership has it downfalls,
Leaving her followers wondering
Who that masked mother was, yet
Always glad she appeared when she did.
But now her pioneering days have ended
And we are now forced to continue on,
Forging our own paths, paving our own roads
But thanks to her our travel will be easier
Because she unselfishly blazed the way.

"Ro-Ro"

Eleven seventeen,
I was born, as was he.
Intriguing how
That came to be.
Not twins, both
Born in different ways.
Eleven seventeen
Being my time, his being the day
But we are still bonded
Closer than the rest,
He's not just a buddy
He is the best.
He is my hero,
My brother, my friend,
Who he has become
I must commend.
Intellectual and driven
Yet down to Earth
It is no wonder why
Angels sang at his birth.
He always works
As hard as he plays,
And to the One above
He often prays.
He's like a chocolate
Milk fountain,
People flock to him
Like the peak of a mountain,

With cups in hand
Wanting a sip of his cool
And just to sit with him
And from him be schooled.
At times I wish I could be
As influential as he,
But naw, I'm content
With simply being me
But I couldn't ask for
A better male sibling,
Though at times
We do get caught quibbling.
Our bond defines
What family is about,
We're there for each other
In all times of doubt.
He is my hero,
My brother, my friend
Born today the
Seventeenth of eleven

"Letter to a Lost Brother"

Dear Brother,
It's me your sister.
I know you are not my full brother,
But just a half-brother.

My father is your father.
My mother is not your mother.

I wish I knew you
But at least I know of you.

You used to come visit before I was born.
I have no memory so my life is torn.

I hope one day before I die,
That we will no longer live a lie,
And come to realize that we are more than just
You and I.

"Christmas Mourning"

I mourn the days
I awoke at 4:30 a.m.
to see the shiny surprise.
The big beautiful green tree
blazing in its glory,
presents tightly tucked
some wrapped in Santa Paper
while the big ones only
ornamented with a bow and a tag...
I mourn awakening the fam and
dragging them to this sight.

I shed tears for the Christmas story
we were "forced" to tell on this morning,
I still hear the screams of pure elation
at the gifts' unwrapping, still look
for the little treats hidden in trees and stockings
while sucking on a red and white cane
and dancing to the Chipmunks Christmas LP.

I miss packing up presents and self
into tiny cars and trekking to Long Island,
Queens, Harlem, the Bronx or wherever the family was.
I miss the hearty meal, food that truly filled the soul.
I miss our griot telling us of his medic and Tank days.
The gifts given and received were never as impressive
nor as important as the box that it was delivered in. I
miss that family connection that superseded all.

I mourn those days,
the days before divorce,
marriage, children and
death raped us of time.
So stretched between
new families, new
responsibilities, new traditions
that this whole was lost,
the family time now
random communications
and reunions at funerals....

I still mourn her,
        but right now...
                I mourn them all...

as I look at the tree I see the vibrant memories
and am reminded of how maliciously
time has twisted this holiday. Nothing
is more violent than change, but with time
it must come, and we must move within
the new circumstances in which we find ourselves.

It started with a child and a marriage
then the snow whited-out one year
and we've never gotten back to the surface,
never got out from under its coating, never
made it back to those days we awakened
anticipating this family gathering...
I mourn for these things, for those
warm embraces on that cold December day...

Is this the end? Have our lives traveled roads
that do not lead back to each other? Will we never
greet again for such a festive occasion?
for such a miraculous birth?....

This is what I think of as I stare
at the tree that's dulled with age...
through eyes that have drowned in their tears...

Yes, I am still thankful for my blessings,
thankful for all the blessings past,
present and yet to come
thankful for the family gifts
that sit under the tree
and though I know
life changes and we must go on
I still mourn
for their presence.
I mourn this Christmas morn.

"United and Still Divided"

We stem from the same ancestry.
Similar blood courses through our veins
Our features and tint even sort of blend...
There is no question as to whether we are kin.
But before we met, before we could seal
The family bond we were split apart.
Ripped away from one another
Before embracing each other
We were forced to live separate lives
With different paths, different views.
We weren't kin that developed the same
But we still ached in our solitary pain
Longing for each other. Needing to be whole
Though our individual lives still progressed.
Your history went one way and mine another.
Neither right nor wrong just a different means
To a similar end, but secretly missing our kin.
Guided by fate, crossed ours roads did
We met, happy to be reunited. You and I
Together for the first time. A chance
To be completed but our ideologies competed.
What was left for me was right to you
And my ups were your downs. Your biases
Clouded your view and my delusions
Kept me from your reality. Though kin,
We were two strangers trying to hug
But without coordination nor communication
As to whether you go over and I go under or
If we should crisscross, meeting in the middle.
Could we forgive what was done to us?
Look past our discrepancies in training
And mend strained bonds, uniting as one?
Could we develop a family, made of
Two varying entities, beliefs and histories?
We tried to meet, both extending arms
In an awkward dance trying to complete
A stymied embrace each becoming frustrated
Eye to eye we could not see, both talking
But neither listening, both unable to ingest
The other's plight. After so long of a fight

It seemed impossible. How could it be
That we, of the same, can differ so much?
A reunion that should have been sweet
Tasted bitter. Two derived from one line,
With the same blood coursing through,
Birthed from the same ancestral tree
Finally reunited still unable to meet.

"Positioned to See"

I get it. Honestly, I get it.
You are pissed at me. Mad
at me for nagging and for
questioning. Frustrated by
the fact that I never seem
satisfied with the man that
you are. I get it. I get how
tiring it must be when I tout
about seeming like a classist.
Seeming as if I think I'm your
superior opposed to your equal,
that I am always looking down
at you just like the world does.
My nose always seems to
touch the clouds with you
never being on my radar. You
are never presentable enough,
never dressed quite right, never
educated enough or making
enough money. It seems as if
you can never be Mr. Do Right.
At least, that's what my
actions have led you to believe.
You think I have no respect.
And, I finally get it. I get it.

You are justified in feeling
how you do. It's true that my
tactics have probably not
helped... I understand that
my unwanted opinions and

unexplained attitudes might
have been the reason why
you opted for the lighter lady,
you know, the one that took
you as is, and you can't see
my problem with our situation,
I wish you could understand
the source of my inspiration
to treat you in such a way,
and it's not based on statistics.
But first I need you to know that
I do get it. I really do see
why you are so displeased

But would you please give me
a moment or two, take time to
listen to why I act as I do? See,
I look to the heavens seeking
my man because he should be
heaven sent. I can't settle for
you as is, because I already
know that you can be more
than this. So when I ask about
your education and occupation,
when I complain about your
vocabulary and style it's because
I see you accepting less, losing
sight of the struggle we were
born into, settling for the prison
mentality that has been keeping
us chained prior to conception.
Understand, that my inquiries
come from a place of freedom.

I plan on going places, I refuse
to be held down. I need to know
if you have the interest and
capability to travel the world
and live this life with me.
I need to know if you can fight
against the odds with me
because I can't be a statistic,

we can't be statistics. I need
to be your prize but often you
are gazing down at my body
not concerned with my mentality.
My worth is not buried in cleavage,
it can't be found in the roundness
of my bottom, you need to look
to the sky to find me, because
that's where I'm trying to get to
in order to meet you. I've been
doing everything to be the best
I can for you, but you step
with your worst or you select
a different shade. But again,

I get it, I get that my persona
makes it hard for you to see
that I am completely devoted.
But right now, we aren't leveled.
Can't see each other, our vision
was lost generations ago and the
more we allow media to tell our story,
the more we refer to ourselves
as simply trifling and hos, means
the longer we will be blinded, but
hear this, I choose you, I always
have. Getting me is easy if you
simply look at me, come to me
properly and I will look at you, then
we finally can drop our defenses,
release our baggage, and just
open our hearts. It is only then
that we will hear that familiar
rhythm, we will be able to deeply
read the purity in our souls and
see that same willingness to fight.
We are each other's reflections
but we will only come to know
this to be true if we finally open
our eyes and are prepared to see.

"Family"

We may not have chosen
the other if given a choice.
Fate may have tricked us
into being together, being a unit.
We may never agree on anything,
we may always be at odds and
never fully appreciate why we
see the world as we do, even if
our stories are bonded by these
same streets, these same walls,
the same ancestors. It matters not
how we interact from day to day
because on that day of need
I'll always be your cheerleader
I will be your supporter and you will
be mine. Even though we might
not be on the same page
we are part of the same book.

Black American

"Dr. King Jr."

Doctor King
Wasn't mean
He fought for black's rights,
Because he knew it was right.
He won the Noble Peace Prize,
Because he was very civilized.
He died a proud man
Even though sadness had spread throughout the land.

"The Public Hearing"

Young, middle, and aged, gathered
in the room. Some to support,
some to defend, some to hate,
others to learn. And despite
the strategic church-like
outbursts, all were respectful,
that is until a light brown one called
a dark brown one an "uncle tom sellout
negro." Ruckus ensued, those that
needed to remain fled, and when
reconvened the air had a stench.
That micro incident emphasized
the macro purpose; to succeed
we must treat each other better.

"Dreams Released"

I stand atop this urban precipice
while tightly gripping my urn of dreams.
It was an old juice can with the words
"dreams deferred" scribbled on the side.
It's where the dusty remnants of
my dreams found their resting place.
My hopes to be a millionaire, the dream
of being a beautician, an interpreter,
inventor, the need for a marriage by
the age of 27, dreams of three children.

This is where I buried my hopes to be
a visual artist, to be a professional
singer or to be a size two. This is where
I left my plans to meet the members
of my favorite boy band, where my
concert hopping hopes resides,
and my desire to direct a Broadway play.

I used to mourn these things and even
bathed this urn in tears on those nights
that I ached for what was never to be
but then, one day, I started to see.
This can was never an urn, only a
place that captured and contained
my vibrant hopes and expectations.

These are not dreams deferred
just the dreams not preferred.
I have made my choices, and
the path that the others would
have led me to, would not have
ended at the me you see. So from
this precipice, high above this
concrete jungle, I release these
dreams that weren't to be, but I
hold on to this one hope, this
one particular dream, that these
that I now release will be captured
and realized by my sisters and
brothers that tragically and
unknowingly forgot
how to fulfill a dream.

"My Peoples Wars"

Who are my people?
And if I identify with them
Does that mean
That I too must fight?
I am black,
A descendent of slaves,
Middle lower class,
And a young Christian
American woman
Supporting alternative lifestyles.
That's a lot to be fighting for.
I'm fighting for oil,
40 acres, and my mule.
I'm fighting to be accepted
In the work force
As a woman
And a black person.
I'm fighting for
women's rights and
marriage equality.
I'm fighting against the atrocities
Done to Native Americans,
And female circumcision
While fighting for the right to vote,
And for equal education.
I must fight for the right
To keep prayer in schools
And for the up keep
Of the Bronx.
I'm fighting against
The Newer "Whiter" Harlem
I am fighting the Man,
Waging a war against the system...
But I'm already worn out
From fighting all of
My people's wars.

"Views on Life Part 3"

Scars are often the
Product of a good
Story; of an interesting
Experience or they
Could be those
Sad reminders of a
Hurt that tragically
Came your way.
They just might be
A visual testament
To your survival and
The courage you possess
But more importantly
Scars are proof
That you lived
Along the way.

"What's Going On?"

What's going on with our world today?
We are all worried and in dismay.

I may not live among the war and crime
But I am not blind and I see what's going on during our time,

When we were young we had not a care
But now it's even dangerous to dare.
We hurt and kill
Just for a thrill.

And I do believe we have achieved
In what many others could not succeed.
We've killed ourselves, our spirit and our soul
All that's left is an empty hole.

What we need now is to unite as one,
To heal the wound and have some fun,
And show those cultures once and for all
That our culture will last through it all.

"America"

America,
"Land of the free", home of the poor.

My ancestors have given their life for you and got nothing in return.

America, you've brought us here, raped us, and forgot us.

America, you say you're great but how can a country that is so great
forget about its own people?

America, you lead others to believe that everyone lives in houses with
picket fences,
yet so many live on the street.

You try to make "America" better than others but in fact you're bettering
only a select part of yourself.

America, you always help suffering countries, but what about helping
the suffering parts of you?

America, when will you stop living this illusion that you're the best
when you're probably the worst?

America, I'm talking to you,
And this time, you better answer me.

"The American Drain"

I step into the shower hopeful that my perfect
petite porcelain American image will restore
itself. But right now, right now my rotund bloated
body is filthy, covered in hate, blood, and guilt. From
split ends to hammer toes, I reek of rancid deeds.

But it's morning now, all mourning must be washed
away with dawn. Wrong doings do not exist today.
We are American. We do no wrong, commit no
harm; we are perfection. Our history books are
testimonies to our greatness. Slaves were willing
workers, the natives happily donated their land for
the manifestly designed plan. Never is it mentioned
that the US established the 1900's campaign for
purity. That was solely Germany's fault. The stealing of
people, the raping of lands, the destruction of culture,
the sterilization of its citizens were all acts washed
down the drain. So why shouldn't I be able to I wash the
blood off of today? Why can't I scrub his name
off my lips? Why can't I rinse this night from my brain?

I curse the day I gave my heart to a stranger only
to have it broken moments later. I hate my mentor
for mentioning his name. Troy. Anthony. Davis.
His story: Wrong choice with wrong people at
wrong time doing wrong things caught in wrong
situations with blue blood spilled permanently.

It was the ambiguity of guilt and the price to be paid
that tugged at my heart. It was a cost too high. A
penalty too stiff for testimonies that changed. Even
his compadre, his partner in crime turned prosecution's
star witness, the blue man's golden boy was overheard
confessing to the deed. A case built on lies, coercion
and circumstantial evidence would cost a life. A life
must not be spared! Justice must prevail! The cop killer
has to die!! Someone has to pay! Who it was and
proof of guilt didn't matter, but they must be black.

Blue fingers pointed in black directions... fingers
pointed indiscriminately discriminately. A familiar
story...Was Troy a Scottsboro Boy? 80 years later
was the South still trying the same case? Had we
learned nothing from the 9 hijacked lives? Or was
it the lesson that black blood must be shed! Eye
for eye, life for life! And the justices were blind and
deaf to the reasonable and resounding pleas.

We screamed, shouted, marched, signed, wrote,
begged and with fists raised and baited breath
we waited. "Don't do this" were the pleas and
prayers of the day. Blood spilled anyway.
Hearts broke worldwide. Tears poured from eyes.
Lynchings were once again legalized.

And while the weight of the night slowed time
and heavy hearts struggled against breathing easy's
impossibility, dawn still came. Day
demanded its place in time and space even if
Troy remains in yesterday, free of bleak tomorrows.
The blood lust satisfied revealing us as bloated and
disgusting/disgusted Americans. The carcass
on our shoulders, blood smeared on our hands
and on our faces, with salt burning our eyes.

But none of this will stay, it will be washed away,
this is America's way. The drain will provide freedom.

So I stand in the shower, I turn on the water, reach
for my loofah, grab my soap and begin the ritual. I
will try to wash away the grotesque image of self.
I will scrub 'til squeaky, 'til porcelain, 'til the scent
of the bewitching hours' stench is gone. The deeds
done at night under flags, we will not speak of.
I scrub. I scrub. And I scrub trying to remove his
blood from my skin, his name from my lips, this
regret filled night from my brain though knowing
this lynching cannot afford be washed away. This
cannot be status quo, cannot be the American way!

"Rhythms and Words"

I've got rhythms and words
Flowing through my head
But I don't know what to write
Because my boy is dead
They beat him to a bloody pulp
Simply because of the words that he wrote
How do I know they won't do the same to me?
How do I know they won't try to kill me?
Over the words that I thought,
The words that that I spoke,
Especially over the words that I wrote?
How do I know?
Is there a guarantee written in stone?
How can I be sure,
That there is safety behind that paper door?
Then again...
For me not to write
Is for me not to exist,
Because writing to me is pure bliss.
So let them beat me any time of the day
'Cause going out doing what I love...
There is no better way.

"The Headline Read"

The headline read:
Should
New Orleans
be rebuilt,
or relocated?

Should New Orleans
be rebuilt?

Should the Government
have to now pay the penalty
for years of neglect and inaction
that could have cost so much less...
Or can they just let this city sink under the sea

washing away all signs of negligence
neatly erasing away the thousands

Thousands.
Thousands lay rotting
covered in blankets on the streets
Thousands are floating
through rivers and waters;
a price so heavily paid simply
because 20 million was too much
for renovations, too much to pay
to keep a happening place okay.

The headline read:
Should New Orleans
be rebuilt or relocated?
Relocated...

It's the Native Americans all over again
Indigenous peoples being sent to reservations,
detached from their true home, populations
that suffered and cultures that died in relocation
a forced divorce from the grounds that bore
and loved them. Could a "new" piece of land
in an overcrowded country really possess the spirit
of those in the rivers, of those that have come and gone?
Would the ground at this new home be saturated with the
smooth jazzish moans that have always resonated?
Will the unfamiliar streets ever be as festive and lively;
will it ever be as warm and embracing? Can it
reproduce or only fabricate that New Orleans magic?

The question "Should New Orleans be rebuilt?"
leaves a bitter taste in my mouth like the bodies
and diseases that now pollutes the air.

Was the lack of renovations on the levees
an oversight or part of an elaborate plan?
A game of political and financial probability.
If it floods *then* profits flow. The natives
will be gone, the land will be more marketable,
filled with nicer places that will cover

the abandoned land, droves of more elite people
imported in that willingly pay for the jazzish
New Orleans lifestyle without any regard
for the original habitants. "Relocation"
the name of the game. The cost? Poor lives
lost that could have been saved.

They could have
          heeded the warnings years prior.
They could have
          created viable disaster plans.
They could have
          abandoned the city when they knew Katrina had chiseled
          "New Orleans" onto the tombstone.
They could have
          sent aid the moment the waters rose past the rim
          and began to flood the bowl.
They could have
          saved the people even though the land was lost.
They could have
          valued the price of a human life.

but instead
          while sleeping
          their lungs
          embraced
          the water
          sealing fates
          of so many
          families
          clinging
          to
          e
          a
          c
          h

          o
            t
                h
                   e
                      r...

and politicians wondered why
the people rioted, why others looted? Why
people regressed to animalistic instincts, why?
Why? Because the country they have loved
and had been loyal to left them to starve,
to die, infested with illness, left with no
food, desperate and that's why the little girl's body
was found with a slit throat. That's why
there were so many shootings in the superdome
and why policemen committed suicide.
Why? The reason? Simple. The government
created that monstrous beast.

This ferocious animal was the backlash of,
the ramifications of, the results of
the Government's nonaction;
the governing body's inaction
that started at the conception of
the hypothesis of this event.

The beast was powered by
people's disenchantment, and
disappointment. It was the physical
manifestation of the resentment,
fear, hunger, confusion and frustration.
Rationale being: If the government
was not going to regulate and aid
then every man for himself, survival the key;
        these were the darkest of hours when this
        vacant ravenous monster looted, raped
        and killed.

These bloody acts, violent deaths
and suffering individuals were created by
the innocent hands of the mayor
        that took too long to evacuate,
by the stable arms of FEMA
        for letting incompetence and red tape slow the aid
and by the warm embrace of the President
        that never confronted the social, racial, economic and emotional
woes.

This thriving American community that
once had a legacy of vibrancy
now looks like a refugee camp
the poor class, now the homeless destitute lost class.

Should New Orleans be rebuilt?
Should it be relocated? Should
we just let the sea like Atlantis
swallow this land that was a huge
part of American Musical History.
Should the Jazz become blues
gurgled up by the sea. Will
the dancers cease to move? Should
the party be wrapped up, ended
for the perpetual night? Should
Katrina win this fight? Should
the city of sinful bliss be
washed away and crumble
like Sodom did? Should
the residents leave the only
homes they've owned?
Should we just forget what
it once all meant?

No, never
for the dancers will
          always be there,
the spirits will
          flood the streets and dance out the end of lent,
the colors will
          always be bright and lively
and the sound will
          always be original, always unique.

And the taste
of the words
New Orleans
(though new)
will again
be sweet.

"The Recipe To Me:"

Start with stolen Africans
place them in a ship shaped
frying pan made in Trinidad,
bring ingredients to simmer.
Add a European or two, some
Natives and a few generations
to the brew. Marinate it in
Carolinian seasoning. Transfer
ingredients to a Northern pot.
Flavor with activists and
entrepreneurs, ministers and
educators, and don't forget
the law makers. Blend and
beat the ingredients, bake
for 35 years at 3 degrees,
plate with complimentary
siblings, top with artistic garnish
bless the meal and then
you've completed the me recipe.

"The Trouble with Labels"

While babysitting me one day my
neighbor ripped my comfortable,
familiar label away. She said that I was not
a true African American. That it belonged
to those like her; those recently born
in Africa and then became American. My
identity demolished. My innocent views
were destroyed. And I carried those
words in my pocket like I do my bubble
gum. Here and there I'd pull it out
and chew on those jagged words, roll them
over my tongue and savor its bitter taste,
but it took maturating, for me to see
that she was just foolishly trivializing
things she knew nothing about. See,
"African American" was created for me,
while "Black" embraces all. It includes

any person of a similar hue whether they
descend from Africa, the West Indies,
or the Latin countries. And though I too
am Black, I am African American first.

I was the one playing with my kin
on my soil when we were ambushed.
I was the one dragged to holding camps
where I first saw what my future would
entail. I can still hear the haunting jingle
of the chains, can hear the whips crackling
through the air. I was the one herded
onto a ship. My body was intermingled
with carcasses for a terrifying eternity
in a cramped, diseased space. When allowed
to see daylight again it was looming over
this hostile land and I was now to be
someone's property, a princess
now made servant. My status was beaten
out of me by my sadistic owners. They,
taught me to mistrust my neighbors,
friends and kin. I, like a wild steed, was
broken and tamed, my name taken away.

A new religion, a new language, and
new way of being were forcibly shoved
down my parched throat to the point
of choking. I hungrily watched my mom
be given away, and then cried as my nursing
babies were ripped violently from my breast.
I was banned from marriage so I jumped
the broom but was still made to breed with
another. My blood dyed the cotton and flavored
the tobacco. I bled at the whipping posts, my
sanctuary ran red when raped by my master, I bled
and bled and cried and bled but no one could hear.

I fled my bondage and slaughtered my
masters with the likes of Nat Turner, I
traveled the train to freedom, I was caught,
beaten and still fled again. I scraped and saved
for my freedom and I carried my emancipation

letter at all times praying it would not be ignored.
And I, once a traveler of the train, became a
railroad stop. This is my legacy, not your history.

You have your own culture, your own beautiful
heritage. I was stripped of mine so I began
to secretly create a new one. I grew my 2/5ths
making me whole. I laid the concrete
that welcomed you to the States. I paved the way
from slave, sharecropper and indentured
servant. I wrote the lyrics to the encrypted
spirituals. I fought in the battles and died
to gain freedom. These buildings, this monopoly
was built on my back. I ignored the Jim Crow laws.
I went to the diners, drank from fountains, I sat
on the bus and would not get up. I was dragged
out, my churches were burnt, crucifixes were
set a blaze fueled by racist rage, I was lynched,
I was the main course at pick-nigs. I
was tarred and feathered made to look like
a chicken but I was not. I was hosed
but my fire never died, I was brutalized but I
still preached love. Though silenced, I still
voted; no one was going to stop me. I had a dream
and it was going to come true by any means!

Without me there would be no filament,
street lights wouldn't exist, sugar and
honey wouldn't be refined. I made the
fire ladder and created blood banks. I made
refrigerators mobile. I invented elevators, hot
combs, gas masks, pencil sharpeners and street
sweepers. I made the steam radiator and the
third rail. I created coin counting tubes
and even helped in the invention of X-rays.

What did you do here? Did you resuscitate
Harlem? Did you write the poems, sing
the music and do the dances? Did you rub
the Tree of Hope? Did you perform in the same
places you were banded from? Were you the first
person of color to enter the hallowed halls

of Oberlin? Were you killed for looking
at a white woman? Did you march with
King and stand with Malcolm? Was it you
that was persecuted here for all those years? No,
but it was my great grandmother that was banned
from reading, my grandparents that only made
it to high school. My mom was the first
to get her degree. Where were you when
this world was changing because of me?

I am rhythm and blues, Hip-hop, and
Gospel. I am the UniverSoul Circus, I am
BET, Ebony and Jet. I am Nguzo Saba. I
celebrate a harvest that I will never see. I am
Affirmative Action, the NAACP and the
Urban League. I am the Black Panthers. I
am the Civil Rights Movement. I am African
American. I eat collard greens, fried chicken,
chitlins, gumbo, black eyed peas, okra, mustard
greens and kale. I am cabbage, gizzards, whiting,
sweet potato pie, stuffing and tongue. I
feast on catfish, barbecue beef ribs, bacon
and grits. These are my traditional foods.

I am Araminta Ross, Tanya Allen, Sojourner
Truth, Madame CJ, Sonia Sanchez, Rosa
Parks, Harriet Jacobs, Toni Morrison, Nikki
Giovanni. I am Marian Anderson, Ms. Baker,
Condoleezza Rice, Mary McCloud Bethune, Shirley
Chisholm, and Dr. Mae Jemison. I am Blanche
Kelso Bruce, Arthur Ashe, Henry Box Brown,
Dr. Drew, Langston Hughes, Crispus Attucks,
Joseph Winters, Leroy Jones, Dred Scott, Mr.
Douglas, Alexander Ashborne, Garrett Morgan,
Countee Cullen. I too sing America and Africa.

I was African, molested and raped by my white
masters. My children were born all shades and
in my search for home, for the familiar, I hid
in the arms of the Native Americans. My skin
is deep yellow, bronze, burnt rust, dark chocolate,
and charcoal. My blood is so mixed that African
American is the only term that can truly define
me and my plight, that can properly name all
the atrocities, and show the strength in whom
I have become. I was African but I cannot go home.
I am now too American, I have forgotten my
native tongue, I cannot go back to which
I have been detached for so very long...

But yet you can come here wearing
my name, saying I am nothing but an
AIDS infested junky, a prostitute and
convict. You say I am lazy and good for
nothing but it was I that opened the door. If
it wasn't for me you would have immigrated
as slave. You'd still be captive at the bottom
of a boat, not comfortably sitting on a plane...
If I am such a disgrace to your tone why
steal my name?... See, by taking my identity
you are only clouding and trivializing a struggle
in which you have no right to claim. Those
acres and that mule are mine, not yours. This plight
is one in which you know nothing about. So
while I will raise my fist and scream "Black
Power!" with anyone of a similar shade
I will not share my African American name.
For I have already lost everything else;
every thing once known to me has been
cruelly taken away. Now cousin, please
don't you join in on this rape too.

"North Carolina"

As I rode through town
I heard the faintest of whispers,
They were almost inaudible
But I heard them.

As I strolled down the vacant streets
Again, an unfamiliar yet very familiar voice spoke to me.
I heard you.

As I stopped for a photo of the cotton field
I felt a welcoming embrace from an uneasy friend,
Trembling at first, then relaxing as it continued.
I felt you.

As I looked at the crumbling stones,
Stumbled on the weeds in that overgrown lot
And I searched tirelessly for your resting place
I talked with you.

As we spoke I learned all there was of you, of me,
And felt you encouraging me to proudly carry on your legacy.
I heard you then and I still hear you.

Epilogue

"When it's all done..."

Do not look at the remnants with pity,
instead celebrate how much I survived.
Every injury, every insult, every attack
only strengthened my resolve to battle on.
So when the battle is done and I rest,
do not list the blows, do not focus
on the things lost, the falters in resolve;
rejoice over my victories, learn from me.
Do not offer pity, I succeeded in being me.

About the Author

As a child, there was nothing Dara hated more than writing, but at the age of nine she was introduced to poetry and that hatred quickly became love. At 16, she started to acknowledge and honor her artistic inclinations. She became a founding member of the Creative Arts Team Youth Theatre and simultaneously started writing poetry on a monthly basis.

Dara holds a BA in Literature with a concentration in Drama Studies from SUNY Purchase. She later received her MA in Educational Theater from NYU and a MPA from Baruch College.

Dara's theatrical career has included the roles of actor, stage manager, and director in numerous community theaters in the northeast region including the HADLEY Players, Teatro LATEA, and Aaron Davis Hall. Under the name Zoetic Fyre, Dara performed on several stages across New York City including Bowery Poetry Cafe and the Nuyorican. She was also featured on WBAI's Perspectives.

Although the idea of this book came to her in 1999 and she has over 800 poems to her name, it wasn't until 2014 that she decided it was time to release her work into the world.

As an artist, Dara believes in addressing the difficult and taboo topics to create discussion, promote healing, and encourage critical thought within her community and across cultures. She is always up for a good conversation but beware, you may plant the seed for her next poem.

Made in the USA
San Bernardino, CA
09 July 2016